Steck-Vaughn
Shutterbug Books
SOCIAL STUDIES

Helen Keller

A Triumph of Spirit

by Jeanne Chally

STECK-VAUGHN
Harcourt Supplemental Publishers

www.steck-vaughn.com

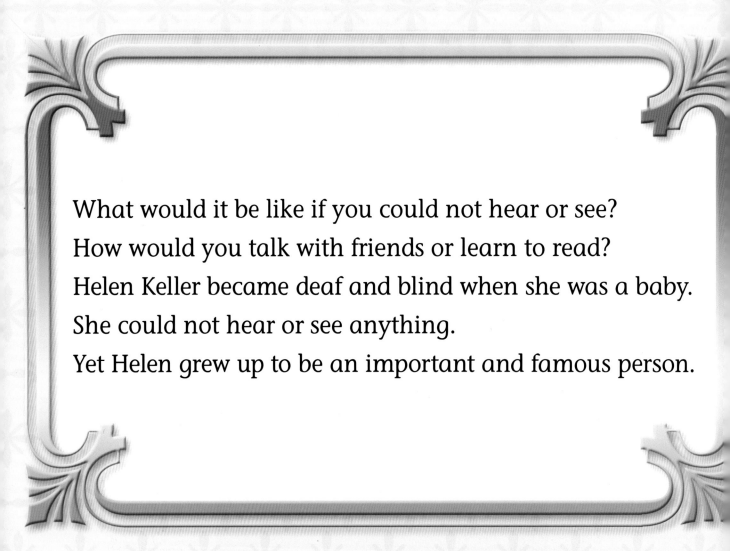

What would it be like if you could not hear or see?

How would you talk with friends or learn to read?

Helen Keller became deaf and blind when she was a baby.

She could not hear or see anything.

Yet Helen grew up to be an important and famous person.

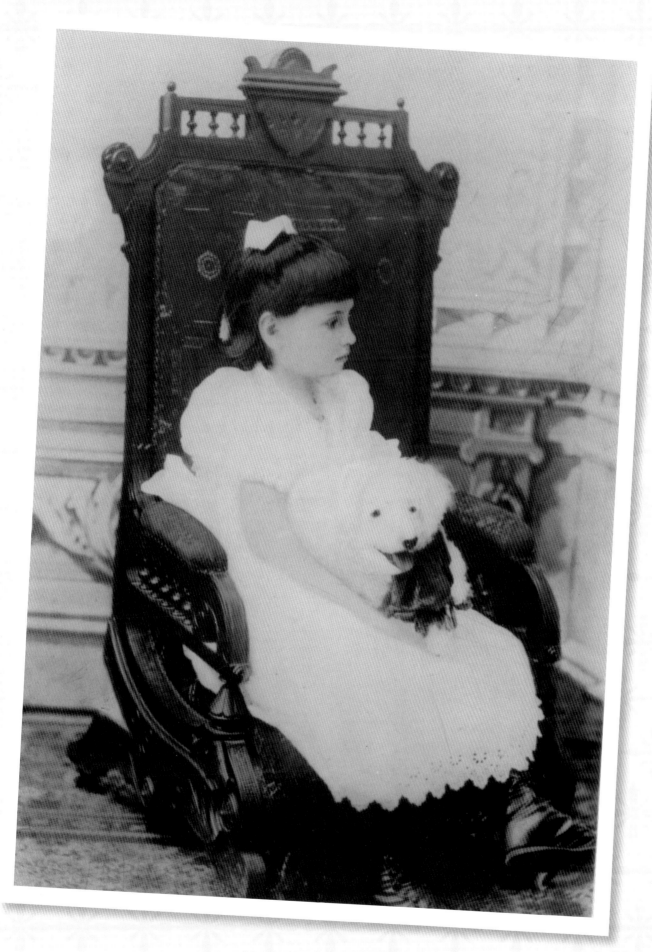

⠩ ⠒⠂ 3

As a young girl, Helen was often scared or angry.
Her family did not know how to talk with her.

When Helen was six years old, a teacher came to help her.
The teacher's name was Anne Sullivan.

Anne taught Helen how to use sign language.
Then Helen could talk by making signs with her hands.

Helen also learned how to read lips.
She understood what others said by feeling their lips move.

Anne taught Helen how to read with her hands.

Helen could read special books with raised dots, or braille.

8

Helen was the first deaf and blind person to go to college.
Anne read Helen books that were not in braille.

Helen loved to learn.

She was one of the best students in her college class.

Helen and Anne worked together for many years.
The student and teacher were friends for life.

Helen wrote books and won many awards.
She worked hard to help people who had special needs.

Helen met many people all over the world.
She even met the President of the United States.

Helen proved that people with special needs can do many things.
With help, Helen found ways to do almost anything.

Helen Keller lived to be 87 years old.

Her life was a triumph of spirit and friendship.

The Alphabet in Sign Language and Braille